Decorating *with* Candles

Decorating *with* Candles

Simon Lycett

Photography by Michelle Garrett

Reader's Digest

The Reader's Digest Association (Canada) Ltd.
MONTREAL

INTRODUCTION

A S A FLORAL decorator and stylist, much of my work involves the use of candles, either incorporated within floral decorations or used in conjunction with arrangements to enhance the mood and create ambiance. Although it takes only a power outage for us to realize just how much we rely on the modern miracle of electricity, there are times when it is refreshing to switch off the glaring electric lights and light a candle instead. Illuminating its surroundings with a much softer, flickering flame, a candle evokes a sense of the past, harkening back to an era when candlelight was an absolute necessity. In Roman times, Pliny the Elder wrote of candles, or rushlights, made from natural rushes, repeatedly dipped and overdipped in tallow (a fat derived from animal carcasses). These were the first solid candles, and

L E F T *Flickering flames have a magical, almost hypnotic quality. Here, a mass of simple votives covers a small garden table, providing a beacon of light as dusk falls.*

superceded the use of oils or liquid fats. These, in conjunction with a wick of cotton or natural rush, were commonly used by all except the very wealthy, who could afford the scarce and expensive commodity of beeswax.

In most of northern Europe, oils were unheard of, and the majority of homes would have been illuminated by candles made from sheep's tallow. At one time, every village would have had a chandler, whose sole occupation was the manufacture of candles. Much as the modern-day utilities are regulated to ensure a proper and efficient supply, so too was the candle maker, whose output was monitored to ensure people were not sold adulterated or shoddy candles.

These early tallow candles burned with a very smoky, smelly flame, sooting up the homes they lit and filling the air and lungs with noxious fumes.

It was not until the late 1800s that progress came, with the advent of the petro-chemical industry to supply fuel for the newly invented combustion-engine powered motor cars. This was when a new form of solid fuel – paraffin wax – became available, from which more refined and cleaner-burning candles could be made.

However, tallow candles are still manufactured specifically for use within some religous organizations, and especially in the Roman Catholic Church where they are a feature of the Requiem Mass. In

BELOW *Large, smooth pebbles, hollowed out to make attractive holders for candles, are ideal for the garden. Because they are heavy, there is no danger of them being blown over.*

BELOW *Most modern candles will not drip, so this household candle was placed in a draft and burned under supervision to create the "dripping" effect.*

many homes though, candles were gradually outshone, first by gaslight and then by electricity. From then on, they were generally reserved for Christmas – when the dusty box of red twisted candles would make a rather dull appearance – or birthdays when candles would decorate the cake.

Candle making became a popular hobby in the 1960s, but it was during the early 1980s that candles began to be featured regularly in home-interiors magazines and were incorporated into interior design by trend-setters who made use of huge, ornate beeswax church candles. Today there are many retail stores, especially those seen in shopping malls, devoted to the sale of candles and associated products. In this book, I hope to inspire you to use candles in your home, not only on special occasions but on an everyday basis. As I write, I have a deliciously scented tuberose candle burning on my workroom desk. At home, supper is always eaten by candlelight; its soft, warming glow is restful to tired eyes needing a break from bright light and the computer screen.

Even though candles are no longer one of life's essentials, they certainly play an important part in creating a welcoming ambiance within the home; whether for a special celebration, a relaxed and informal evening with family and friends, or a solitary time for reflection and peace. Their warm, flickering light can even soothe the soul and uplift the spirits.

BELOW Plain, store-bought candles are fun to decorate – you can turn them into designer items by embellishing them with a few pretty flower petals or leaves.

BELOW In addition to looking beautiful, scented candles release their fragrance as they burn, perfuming the air with a subtle, fresh scent.

MATERIALS & EQUIPMENT

*T*HERE ARE VERY few materials and items of equipment needed to make a basic candle – in fact, all you really need is some paraffin wax, a little dye, a mold, and a primed wick in order to create an attractive decoration. Once you begin to experiment, and as you progress through the projects in this book, you will come across all the items listed below. Another handy accessory for the candle decorator, not mentioned here because it is not essential, is a glue gun, which can be purchased from most hardware or craft stores.

PARAFFIN WAX

Manufactured as a by-product of the oil refining and petro-chemical industries, paraffin wax is sold in large flat sheets or in granules, and forms the basis for the majority of candles. White when solid, it melts at a temperature of between 104-160°F (40-71°C), becoming a clear colorless liquid. It burns well, with a clean, odorless flame. Usually, you will need to add stearin to paraffin wax, although it can be bought with 10 percent stearin already added.

STEARIN

This grainy, hard wax comes in tiny granules and looks like laundry powder. It is added to paraffin wax when making a candle in a mold because it causes the wax to shrink slightly, allowing the candle to be removed from the mold more easily. Used in a ratio of one part stearin to ten parts paraffin wax, the stearin should be melted first, and the paraffin wax added to it. If too much stearin is added, it can give the finished candle a soap-like appearance.

BEESWAX

Entirely natural, this wax is made by bees, forming the comb in which the honey is stored. It is the most expensive of all the waxes and is available in granules in natural amber shades or bleached creamy white. It has a wonderful scent, making it well worth the expense. Beeswax is often used with other waxes to prolong their burning time, but it can be sticky, so if more than 10 percent of beeswax is used for a molded candle, a releasing agent should be applied to the mold first.

BEESWAX SHEETS

Beeswax can also be bought by the sheet, in natural, bleached, or dyed shades, which can be rolled up around a length of unprimed wick to form an attractive candle. Make sure that you save any leftover or torn sheets to add to ordinary wax to prolong its burning time.

THERMOMETER

When making candles, the wax will need to be heated to certain temperatures. You can buy special wax thermometers, but you could also use an ordinary cooking thermometer, provided it covers the same range of 100-225°F (38-108°C).

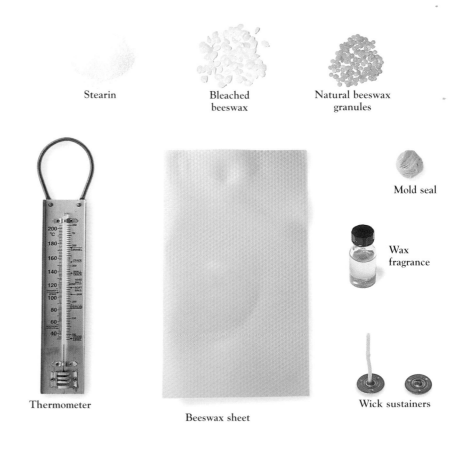

Stearin

Bleached beeswax

Natural beeswax granules

Mold seal

Wax fragrance

Thermometer

Beeswax sheet

Wick sustainers

MOLD SEAL

A putty-like material, mold seal is used to ensure that molds are watertight, and can be reused many times.

WAX FRAGRANCE

Specifically made to scent candle wax, a few drops of fragrance should be added to the molten wax. Avoid adding too much because most perfumes are highly concentrated. Essential oils serve the same purpose, although some do not give off a very appealing smell when burned. Wax fragrances can also be used to scent wicks – a better option if making candles in plastic or rubber molds as fragrances tend to taint these materials.

WICK

A wick is a means of allowing wax vapor to form from molten wax, for it is the vapor that burns and forms the flame. Generally made from woven cotton, wicks are often treated with chemicals to help them burn. The size of the wick is very important, as it will affect how the candle burns: a ratio of a 1in (2.5cm) wick for a 1in (2.5cm) diameter candle is the general rule. Unless making rolled beeswax candles, all wicks should be primed before use (see page 12). Primed wicks can be stored flat between sheets of wax paper in a shallow box.

WAX DYES

Wax can be dyed all sorts of colors using wax dyes. These are sold in disc and powder form, with discs being by far the easiest to use. Follow the manufacturer's instructions for quantities needed. When you require an accurate shade, it is wise to make up a test batch in advance and wait until it sets to see the true color. A word of warning: the powdered wax is highly concentrated and will dye everything in its path if spilled!

WICKING NEEDLE

Available in a variety of sizes, a wicking needle is used for inserting wicks as well as for securing the wick when preparing a mold (see page 12).

WICK SUSTAINER

Used to support the wick when a candle is made in a container, this tiny metal disc has a pierced central hole, through which the primed wick is pushed. The metal is then pressed down so it sits flat in the base of the container.

MOLDS

Glass, perspex, rubber, and plastic molds are available in many extraordinary shapes, patterns, and sizes. My favorite molds are rigid perspex or plastic ones, because they give the smoothest, glossiest finish. However, they can crack if not treated carefully. Rubber molds can produce candles with interesting surface detailing, but will wear out after extended use.

DOUBLE BOILER

Wax should never be melted over a direct heat, so a double boiler is essential. You can improvise by using two stainless steel or aluminum saucepans. Boil the water in the bottom saucepan and melt the wax in the top one, always making sure that the water does not boil dry.

PLASTICIZER

Used in small quantities, plasticizer is an opaque substance that is added to wax to increase burning time and improve the appearance of the candle.

Pyramid mold

Square mold

Unprimed wick

Wicking needle

Wax dye disc

Plasticizer

Powdered wax dye

Double boiler

Paraffin wax

BASIC TECHNIQUES

CANDLES ARE ACTUALLY very easy to make, and once you have mastered the basic techniques shown below, you can use them to create a whole range of decorative candles in any shape or form. As you become more experienced, you will discover that a whole range of effects can be achieved – and even if your experiments fail, you can always melt the wax down again and start over! The projects do not specify the quantity of wax, or dye, required, because this will vary each time according to how large a candle you want to make. As a general rule, though, you can work out the quantity needed by filling the mold with water and measuring it. For every $3^1/_2$ floz (100ml) of water, you will need approximately 3oz (90g) of cold wax. If you do melt too much wax, just put it to one side and leave it to set – you can then melt it again when needed.

PRIMING A WICK
Heat some paraffin wax to 160°F (71°C), then remove it from the heat. Fold a length of wick in two, or tie a loop in the end so it can be hung up. Lower the wick into the wax for 30 seconds, or until air bubbles stop rising to the surface. Remove the wick, pull it tight, then hang it up to

DYEING WAX
Melt your measured quantities of stearin and paraffin wax. Cut a piece of wax dye disc into crumbs (the quantity needed depends on the depth of color required, see Wax dyes, page 11). Remove the wax from the heat and stir in the dye crumbs with a wooden skewer until completely dissolved.

PREPARING A MOLD
Thread a length of primed wick through the hole at the base of the mold and secure it with masking tape. (The base of the mold will become the top of the candle when it is turned out.) Press mold seal firmly around the hole to prevent any leakage, then wind the other end of the wick around a skewer or wicking needle and rest it on top of the mold so the wick is centrally positioned.

USING HOUSEHOLD ITEMS AS MOLDS
Many containers found around the house, and even the garden, make ideal candle molds, provided they are made from suitable, heat-resistant material and have a smooth interior.

SAFETY ADVICE

• When melting wax over heat, never leave it unattended – wax is as dangerous as hot cooking fat or oil and can quickly and easily catch fire.

• Always keep lit candles out of drafts and away from curtains, lampshades, and other fabrics and furnishings.

• Position candles on a flat, stable surface where they are unlikely to be knocked over. Be aware that a candle flame gives off a surprising amount of heat – so do not place a candle directly underneath an overhanging shelf.

• Never leave children unsupervised around burning candles.

• If flowers, leaves, or any other flammable materials form part of the candle decoration, extinguish the candle flame before it burns down to within 1in (2.5cm) of the decoration.

• Always use a flame-retardant spray when using flammable materials in conjunction with candle displays.

A B O V E *These three candles – one square, one rectangular, and one pyramid in shape – were made using perspex molds, which give a wonderfully shiny and smooth finish. Each was poured from the same batch of wax, with more wax dye being added in between pourings.*

Plain and Colored Candles

BASIC CANDLES, consisting solely of plain or colored wax, are simple to make. Rolled beeswax candles are the most rudimentary of all, as they consist entirely of sheets of natural beeswax that have been rolled up by hand without the need for any special equipment. The golden color of natural beeswax has a wonderfully mellow quality, while sheets of colored beeswax can look highly dramatic and can achieve many interesting effects. Molded colored candles are also fun to create and provide an ideal starting point for the novice candlemaker.

ABOVE *This conical "tutti-frutti" candle, made from chunks of lime green and yellow wax, would be perfect for a conservatory or sunroom.*

LEFT *Simple but beautiful, beeswax candles have a warm, natural color and exude a sweet fragrance.*

15

BEESWAX CANDLES

SECRETED BY BEES and used to construct their honeycombs, unbleached beeswax has a beautiful, natural warm amber coloring and a wonderful aroma. It is used in artificial fruit, cosmetics, ointments, and floor waxes, though I tend to use it in just two ways – for polishing the furniture – or most importantly, when making candles, as this is when its color and smell can be enjoyed fully. Thin sheets of beeswax have all the translucent qualities of honeycomb, along with its characteristic pattern. This is probably the easiest way of making candles, because the sheets are easily available from specialist candlemaking suppliers and many art and craft stores.

MAKING THE BEESWAX CANDLES

For each candle, you will need:
1 sheet of beeswax; craft knife; metal ruler; length of medium wick; sharp scissors; and a hairdryer (optional).

When buying sheets of beeswax, check that they are all intact with no broken edges because any cracks or tears will be tricky to repair.

1 Cut a length of wick to fit the sheet and extend it for lighting at one edge by an inch or so. Soften the wax for rolling if necessary by gently applying heat from a hairdryer.

2 Roll the sheet up around the wick, working away from your body and applying fairly firm pressure as you roll. Use your fingers to make sure that the base of the candle remains level.

3 When the rolling is complete, use the pad of your thumb to press the edge of the sheet into the candle, making a neat, firm, and smooth join.

4 Trim the wick to a length of ³/₄in (2cm). Work a small piece of wax between your fingers until it is soft and then wrap around the wick to "prime" it, ready for burning.

NATURAL BEESWAX CANDLES
Plain, naturally colored beeswax candles have a simplicity that needs little enhancement, particularly when their wonderful perfume fills the air.

COLORED BEESWAX CANDLES

Colorful alternatives can be created by simply wrapping additional sheets of beeswax around the original candle.

Rolling two sheets of different colored beeswax together, at an angle, produces an effect that is altogether different and fun. You will have to use a sharp knife to cut across the base to make sure it is straight.

RIGHT *The reds, pinks, and greens of these straight and pyramid-shaped candles make a vibrant group, which would look beautiful arranged on a side table.*

CHUNKY GRAVEL CANDLE

*B*OLD AND STRIKING, this is a modern candle inspired by the seventies. Slightly outrageous and wonderfully loud, it would be ideal for a party. To give the wax its distinctive color, you will need to use wax dye (see Equipment and Techniques, pages 10-13). Wax crayons and even some poster paints will also dye wax, although these may make the candle burn with a sooty flame. As always, learning how to create the desired effect comes with experience. A few words of warning: be extremely careful if using powdered wax dye because it is highly concentrated (one teaspoonful will dye several pounds of wax) and, if spilled, is virtually impossible to clean up. The candle is coated in multicolored aquarium gravel, which can be found in most good pet stores.

MAKING THE CHUNKY GRAVEL CANDLE

You will need: multicolored aquarium gravel (or you can buy single colors of gravel and blend them yourself); paraffin wax; wax dye; saucepan (or similar container to act as a mold); double boiler; large bowl; primed wick; masking tape; scissors; and a skewer.

To help the gravel mould to set, remove the pan after forming a hollow in the gravel and place the bowl in the freezer for a few hours. Moistening the gravel will also help it hold its shape before the wax is poured in.

1 Half-fill a large bowl with gravel. Using a saucepan, form a hollow in the center of the gravel to act as the mold for the wax. Remove the saucepan carefully, trying not to disturb the surrounding gravel.

2 Before pouring wax into the mold, measure a length of primed wick from the base of the hollow to the top of the bowl and trim to size. You will need a total of four wicks of equal length.

3 Melt the wax, add wax dye, and pour the mixture into the mold until it is half-full. Pour the wax over the back of a thermometer or spoon so the gravel does not move.

4 Place two lengths of tape across the mold. Punch four holes in the tape with a skewer and thread the trimmed wicks through – the tape will suspend the wicks and prevent them from sinking into the wax. Fill with the remaining wax.

5 Leave the candle to set for about three hours before removing it from the mold. The gravel will stick to the wax, forming a coating on the outside of the candle. Neaten the finished candle by brushing off excess lumps of gravel.

TUTTI-FRUTTI CANDLE

*T*HIS IS AN IMMENSELY satisfying candle to make, and it demonstrates just how easy it is to transform a few scraps of colored wax into a stunning new candle. It is an excellent way of using up the ends of candles that have burned down, or any materials left over from other candlemaking projects. With a little practice, you can experiment with a whole range of shades to coordinate with the color scheme of a room or a table setting. Here I opted for a soft pastel look, using shades of pink, yellow, green, and blue, and a rectangular mold to create a candle that looks a little like a block of tutti-frutti ice-cream. You can also achieve dramatic results by mixing a range of very bold colors, or perhaps two or more shades of one color.

MAKING THE TUTTI-FRUTTI CANDLE

You will need: candle mold; double boiler; paraffin wax; stearin; primed wick; wicking needle; mold seal; masking tape or adhesive tape; sharp knife; plasticizer; large jar or deep basin; and weights.

Plasticizer increases the translucency of paraffin wax and gives this candle added luster (see Materials & Equipment, pages 10-11).

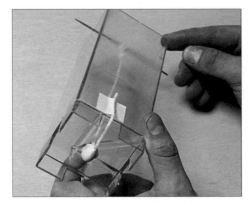

1 Insert a primed wick through the hole in the mold, tie it around a wicking needle, and rest the needle on the open end of the mold. Pull the other end of the wick taut, trim it, and then tape it to the side of the mold. Press mold seal around the top of the mold and check that it is watertight.

2 Cut up colored wax into small chunks and drop the pieces into the mold. Leave about ³/₄in (2cm) at the top to allow room for the molten wax.

3 Melt the stearin and paraffin wax in the double boiler until it resembles clear liquid. Pour the mixture into the mold, and then leave it to settle for several minutes.

4 Using the back of a spoon, gently tap around the outside of the mold to encourage any air bubbles in the wax to rise to the surface.

5 Fill a container with water so when you place the mold into it, the water will come to within ¹/₂in (1cm) of the top. Place weights on top of the mold and leave to cool.

20

REMOVING THE CANDLE MOLD

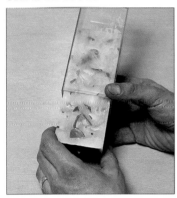

After about three hours, the candle should be ready to be removed from the mold. Tap the sides of the mold gently to help loosen the wax, then slide the candle out and trim the wick with scissors.

RIGHT

This fruit cocktail of a candle looks almost good enough to eat! It is made by pouring regular paraffin wax over multicolored chunks of wax.

Scented Candles

*T*HERE ARE LITERALLY *hundreds of scented candles sold in department stores these days, from those perfumed with natural essential oils and essences to those with more synthetic floral, fruity, or even food aromas. When buying scented candles, it is advisable to spend that little bit extra, because you really do get what you pay for. Cheaper candles may have been perfumed with inferior scents and tend to burn very quickly, with a dirty flame. Fortunately, it is very easy to create scented candles yourself, choosing your own favorite natural aromas.*

A B O V E *Slices of dried preserved lime, used to decorate this citrus-scented candle, are illuminated by the flickering flame.*

L E F T *Floral-fragranced candles can smell almost as good as real flowers, and form an attractive display within glass and porcelain containers.*

CINNAMON CANDLE

*A*LTHOUGH I HAVE used a store-bought candle for the base of this decoration, you could make your own if you have the time. Once you have the basic candle, it is very quick and easy to add cinnamon sticks around the outside, which are supported by a coating of scented wax. I love the light scent of cinnamon – even in concentrated form it never seems oppressive – and as well as looking attractive, these sticks make perfect

decorations for a candle because they are relatively robust. The wax is scented with cinnamon fragrancing oil, and because the cinnamon sticks are warmed up by the flame, they too will give off a discreet perfume.

There are many interesting effects to be achieved using this technique: seashells and pebbles look wonderful set within the wax casing, as do beads, marbles, and even seed pods and small pieces of bark.

MAKING THE CINNAMON CANDLE

You will need: smooth plastic surface (the base of an upturned plastic bowl or tub is ideal); 15 sticks of cinnamon, at least 5in (12cm) long; candle, about 5in (12cm) tall and 2in (6cm) in diameter; heavy-duty aluminum foil, such as a piece cut from an empty soft-drink can; 10oz (280g) beeswax; cinnamon wax fragrance; double boiler; and a metal spoon with insulated handle.

Use a knife to pare off any mold seal stuck to the base of the candle when you remove it from the mold.

MAKING THE MOLD

Bend a sheet of aluminum foil (cut to the same depth as the candle) into a cylinder shape, about 2½in (7cm) in diameter. Secure it to a flat base (here I have used the bottom of an upturned plastic bowl) using mold seal. Press the mold seal all the way around the base of the cylinder to form a seal between the foil and the plastic bowl. Make sure that the seal is watertight by pouring in a little water. Check it does not leak, then pour out the water and let dry.

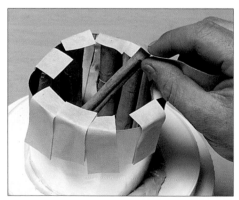

1 Line the inside of the aluminum mold with cinnamon sticks, cut to the correct height for the mold. Secure the cinnamon sticks in place by sticking them to the outside of the mold with masking tape.

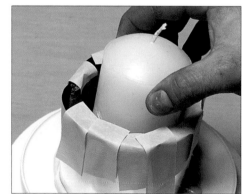

2 Place a candle into the center of the aluminum mold – using a store-bought candle saves time and effort since you do not need to prime and add a wick, or wait for the candle to set.

3 Melt the beeswax, add cinnamon fragrance, and pour the molten mixture into the gap between the candle and the wall of the aluminum mold. Leave for at least three hours to allow the wax to set.

24

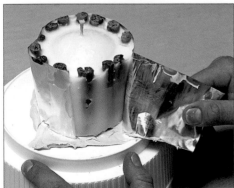

4 After the candle has set, peel back the aluminum and remove the candle from its plastic base. You may need to be firm, since the seal is very sticky.

5 To finish off the candle, heat a spoon in boiling water and then use the back to soften and rub off any wax that is covering the cinnamon sticks.

A B O V E *This easy-to-make candle is placed on a terracotta saucer, which complements the earthy color of the cinnamon sticks. As the candle burns, its sweet cinnamon perfume is released into the air.*

VANILLA BUCKETS

*T*HESE SIMPLE, SCENTED candles will gently perfume the room with the crisp, clean aroma of vanilla pods, almost as if someone had just cooked a delicious pound cake! Because molds can sometimes be tainted by essential oils, I have used miniature galvanized buckets as containers. Keep in mind that when the candle is lit, you should always place the metal bucket on a heat-resistant surface because it will become hot. For this candle I opted for a commercially available candle fragrance, which I added to the wax. If you are using a mold, you should scent the candle by adding fragrance to the wick, as this will not affect the container. To do this, simply add a few drops of wax fragrance as you are priming the wick (see Basic Techniques, page 14).

MAKING THE VANILLA BUCKETS

You will need: galvanized steel buckets; double boiler; paraffin wax; wax fragrance or essential oil; primed wick; wicking needle; and a wick sustainer.

Essential oils may be used instead of commercial wax fragrance oils, but they can clog the wick and produce soot, whereas the specially produced oils are cleaner. If you are making a whole batch of scented candles, perhaps with different fragrances, you can label them. This way you can make sure that you only light compatible scents at the same time to prevent the aromas from being too overpowering.

1 Trim a length of primed wick to just below the holes in the bucket. Support the wick with a wick sustainer and place it in the center of the container.

2 Pour 1in (2.5cm) of molten wax into the bottom of the bucket and let it set. This cements the wick holder to the base to keep the wick in place.

3 Add a few drops of your chosen fragrance or oil to the molten wax and stir to make sure the mixture is well blended. Be careful not to add too much fragrance to the wax, since some are highly perfumed.

4 Support the wick by attaching it to a wicking needle that rests over the bucket. Then pour in the perfumed wax, remembering to stop short of any decorative holes in the container (as seen here) and leave to set. Shrinkage may occur while the wax is setting, so you may need to add extra wax if necessary.

ABOVE *These charming galvanized buckets are filled with*
wax that has been perfumed with candle fragrance.
As they burn, they perfume the air with the fresh, delicate
scent of vanilla pods.

27

ORANGE CANDLE

*L*OOKING JUST LIKE a jar of delicious, homemade orange marmalade, this candle has a fresh, tangy, orange fragrance. Orange-scented wax fragrance is added to the paraffin wax, along with a little plasticizer to aid translucency. The addition of several preserved orange slices and grated orange-colored wax "peel" gives it that extra orangey feel. Dried fruit slices can be found in any good flower shop or craft store, while the "peel" is grated from a block of orange molding wax using a cheese grater. This is then frozen until you are ready to add it to the mold. Freezing the grated wax helps it to retain its shape once the molten wax is added, but it must be placed in an airtight container – if ice gets into the wax, it will cause water pockets within the finished candle.

MAKING THE ORANGE CANDLE

You will need: square glass jar or vase, about 5in by 5in (12cm by 12cm); paraffin wax; stearin; double boiler; four dried orange slices; 2in (5cm) cube of orange molding wax; orange-colored wax dye; orange-scented wax fragrance or essential oil; primed wick; wick sustainer; wicking needle or wooden skewer; and plasticizer.

1 Trim a primed wick to the height of the container plus $^1/_2$ in (1.5cm), and insert one end into a wick sustainer. Support the wick with a wicking needle or skewer and pour in a little molten wax to hold the sustainer in place.

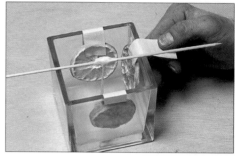

2 Using masking tape, attach a slice of dried orange to the inside of each side of the glass container, so the orange is about $^3/_4$-1in (2-3cm) below the rim.

3 Grate the orange molding wax on the large holes of a standard cheese grater – when added to the candle the grated wax will give the appearance of marmalade. Because molding wax is very soft, place the gratings in the freezer for about one hour before use, to ensure that they hold their shape.

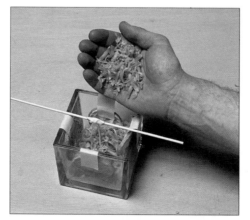

4 Place a couple of large handfuls of frozen grated orange wax into the container – the jar should be no more than two-thirds full in order to leave enough room for the molten wax to be poured in.

5 Melt the paraffin wax and add the orange fragrancer. Pour the wax into the jar so it covers the tops of the oranges, and leave the candle to set for 15 minutes. Once a skin has formed on the top of the candle, the masking tape can be removed without disturbing the orange slices.

Candles for the Dining Room

CANDLES COMPLEMENT any table setting and, displayed in novel and unusual ways, make stunning centerpieces. A summer dinner party will look lovely and fresh if the candles are arranged to reflect the menu – green beans, asparagus spears, pineapples, or limes, for example, make original candle-holders for ordinary candles. A candelabra, adorned with fresh flowers, adds a special touch to a romantic dinner, while a fruit-filled, candlelit ice bowl steals the limelight at a buffet party.

A B O V E   *Shiny red and orange peppers make original and striking candleholders at a summer dinner party.*

L E F T   *Little green beans have the right curves to form raised candleholders, limes are used whole and sliced, and an artichoke makes another interesting holder.*

31

EDIBLE CANDLEHOLDERS

THESE ORIGINAL but highly effective decorative candleholders are always very popular with people giving parties on a slightly more informal or unusual theme. In fact, I was recently asked to design the decorations for a vegetarian dinner party and the entire table was adorned with vegetables of all kinds, inclucing asparagus. Although the spears can often be rather expensive, after the party is over, the asparagus can still be cut from the candle, washed, and cooked in the usual way. If asparagus is not available, it may be substituted with any number of alternative vegetables and fruits that are strong enough to support the candles. Stems of rhubarb, green beans, slim carrots, or even baby zucchini all work equally well.

MAKING THE EDIBLE CANDLEHOLDERS

You will need: 20-30 asparagus spears, depending on their thickness; thick candle, about 10in (25cm) long and 3½in (8cm) in diameter; twine; sharp knife; and a cutting board.

When adding the asparagus, make sure that none overlap – they should form a neat line so you do not end up with a lumpy finish. Place the candle securely on a heat-resistant surface before lighting it and reserve the asparagus leftovers to make a tasty soup!

1 Bind a handful of asparagus to the candle, holding the asparagus in place with one hand and using the other to wrap twine around the candle.

2 Add more handfuls of asparagus, binding them to the candle with several loops of twine until the candle is covered. Aim to work with 5-6 stems at a time because trying to add any more in one attempt is unmanageable.

3 Tie the garden twine securely to keep the asparagus in place. Place the candle on a cutting board and, using a sharp knife, cut off the ends of the asparagus spears so they are level with the base of the candle.

MAKING THE PINEAPPLE HOLDERS

Slice off the bottom of the pineapple to make a level base. Pull out some of the central leaves to make room for the candle to be inserted, and then slip in a candle.

FRUIT-FILLED ICE BOWL

THE COMBINATION OF fire and ice is a magical one, especially when these two opposites look as good and as fresh together as they do here. I have always loved the effect created by light passing through ice, and ice bowls – whether filled with fruit, flowers, herbs, or sequins – are a great favorite of mine. Perhaps it is their transient nature that makes them so appealing; although this decoration would not last throughout an entire dinner party, it would certainly make a novel and stylish addition to the coffee tray, or a beautiful way to serve hors d'oeuvres or drinks at a summer garden party. Whatever the occasion, the fact that you have gone to the effort of preparing this special ice bowl is sure to be appreciated by your guests.

MAKING THE FRUIT-FILLED ICE BOWL

You will need: large glass bowl; smaller bowl to fit inside first bowl leaving a gap of at least 2in (5cm); water-resistant adhesive tape; assorted small summer fruit, such as blueberries, cranberries, cherries, raspberries, and strawberries; water pitcher; 4-5 floating candles; and glitter or sequin stars (optional).

Fruits like raspberries and strawberries are not as dense as cherries and blueberries. This means that the former will tend to float to the surface, so the heavier berries should be added first.

1 Arrange a layer of cherries in the bottom of a large glass mixing bowl, then pour over just enough water – about 1in (2.5cm) – to cover the fruit.

2 Place a smaller bowl on top of the cherries inside the glass bowl. Make sure the smaller bowl is centrally positioned, and then secure it in place using tape at regular intervals between the two bowls.

3 Fill the gap between the two bowls with assorted fruit. The fruit can be built up in layers, or added randomly. Do not pack the fruit too tightly because space is needed for the water. Glitter may also be added to the bowl at this stage to provide extra sparkle.

4 After all the fruit has been added, fill the gap between the two bowls with water, until level with the rims of the bowls. Place in a freezer and leave for 12 hours, or preferably overnight, until completely frozen.

5 Once frozen, remove the ice bowl from the two containers by running the outside bowl under warm water for a minute to loosen it and then sliding the ice bowl out. Fill the ice bowl with water and add floating candles.

ABOVE *This sparkling ice bowl, filled with luscious summer
berries, makes a fresh and delicious decoration for any table. The
crisp, white, floating candles contrast starkly with the richness of the
berries encapsulated within a thick wall of ice.*

35

ROMANTIC CANDELABRA

*W*HAT COULD BE MORE romantic than wining and dining by candlelight – especially when champagne, oysters, and red roses are all part of the occasion? Here, a multitude of red roses is teamed with other rich, jewel-colored flowers to create an opulent and vibrant decoration, incorporating thick, deep purple candles. The base for this decoration is a tabletop candelabra, made specifically to hold fresh flowers and candles and available from florists' suppliers and some art and craft stores. You could also improvise with an ordinary candelabra by making a chicken-wire cage to support the florists' foam. I have teamed classic red roses with clashing pink and purple blooms for a striking color combination, but you may prefer using flowers in pretty pastel shades.

MAKING THE
ROMANTIC CANDELABRA

You will need: candelabra that will contain candles securely; soaked florists' foam; chicken wire; florists' wire; candles; selected seasonal foliage and flowers; and ribbon in a shade that coordinates with the flowers.

As a precaution, treat the ribbon with flame-retardant spray before use.

Stems of thick and woody foliage should be snipped off at the base and split by about ½in (1.5cm) to help them take up water from the foam.

1 Immerse the florists' foam in a bowl or bucket of water and leave to soak until it sinks. Place the soaked foam into the candelabra bowl and secure it with chicken wire and florists' wire.

2 Insert stems of assorted foliage into the florists' foam. The goal is to completely cover the foam and wire, while building a roughly spherical and uniform shape.

3 Add the fresh flowers, inserting them deeply into the foam so they are secure and can take up water. Keep in mind that they should not come too close to the tops of the candles.

4 Make up four small bunches of flowers and foliage, secure them with stub wires, and attach each to the base of a candle with ribbon.

5 Position the candles on the sconces securely. Do not let the candles burn within 1in (3cm) of the flowers or foliage.

Candles for the Living Room

GLOWING FROM BEHIND *attractive woven copper, tin, and brass shades, or presented inside lighter, fresher holders, made from translucent wax with sprigs of herb or flower petals set within the wax, candles give an extra dimension to the living room, immediately evoking a feeling of welcome, warmth, and wellbeing. Even on dark, gray days, by closing the curtains and lighting a few candles you can create a cozy haven in which to sit back with a good book or enjoy the company of friends.*

A B O V E   *Within a cube created from thin sheets of white wax holding fragrant herbs and leaves, a simple candle casts a fresh and atmospheric light.*

L E F T   *A golden glow emanates from this woven copper and aluminium shade, which is placed over a nightlight.*

GLASS CHANDELIER

SPARKLING AND ELEGANT, this wonderfully decorative candleholder has an element of kitsch, but would look great hanging in any room of the house, or perhaps suspended from a tree during an *al fresco* dinner party. I have always admired the immense and opulent Venetian glass chandeliers, and my tribute to these grand ornamentations is made using rather less expensive materials and a minimum of equipment. In fact, needle-nose pliers and wire cutters are the only tools required. I have opted to use clear and mirror-finished glass beads, giving the chandelier a sophisticated, yet sparkling clean look. However, colored beads, whether you choose complementary shades or a complete contrast of bright colors, will give a more dramatic effect.

MAKING THE GLASS CHANDELIER

You will need: approximately 12¹/₂ft (3.75m) of ¹/₁₆in (1.5mm) galvanized fencing wire; needle-nose pliers; wire-cutters; thin silver beading wire; quantity of glass beads with a central hole large enough to allow them to be threaded onto the galvanized wire; and selected glass beads in the size and color of your choice.

Galvanized fencing wire, which is relatively easy to bend, is sold by the reel at most hardware stores.

1 Cut five 22in (55cm) lengths and one 3ft (1m) length of galvanized wire. Bend the longest wire in half and twist the ends together tightly – this will act as the main support.

2 Twist each of the five arms onto the support wire, leaving 10cm (4in) free at the top and 5cm (2in) at the base. Twist the arms in different directions to make them look more interesting.

3 Thread glass beads onto the top wire arms and use a dot of glue to stick the end beads in place. With the pliers, curl the ends of these beaded arms inwards into spiral shapes. Then thread more beads onto the bottom arms.

4 Bend the lower arms into shape, finishing each with a corkscrew spiral to act as the candleholder. Thread beads onto lengths of silver wire and attach them randomly to the lower branches and the central support.

5 To finish off the chandelier, form a tassel from a long length of tiny beads (or buy a suitable beaded trimming from a department store) and attach it to the base of the main support with silver reel wire.

WOVEN COPPER SHADE

*W*HEN I FIRST came across these brass, aluminum, and copper sheets in a craft store, I was very excited at the prospect of experimenting with new materials. I discovered that they have an excellent sheen and color and are also fairly strong, so they can be manipulated into all sorts of interesting and attractive shapes. One drawback is that they tend to dent and scratch very easily, so care must be taken when handling them. The metal sheets are also thin, which means they can easily be cut using sharp scissors – be warned, however, that the edges are extremely sharp.

Copper, brass, and aluminum are all particularly suited to use with candlelight because they reflect the warm glow of a flame and enhance its color.

MAKING THE WOVEN COPPER SHADE

You will need: one sheet each of copper, aluminum, and brass, 14in (35cm) long and 6$\frac{1}{2}$in (16.5cm) wide; ballpoint pen; ruler; scissors; bradawl; copper reel wire; and a cutting board.

These copper shades should be used over votive candles contained within glass holders, or over thick pillar candles supported on small stands.

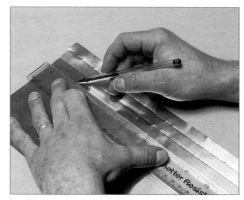

1 Using a ballpoint pen and ruler, measure out and mark a series of lines, spaced $\frac{1}{2}$in (1.5cm) apart, running parallel to the longest edge of the sheet of copper. Press firmly, but be careful not to puncture the copper.

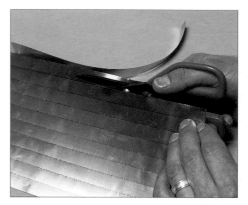

2 Divide the copper into strips by cutting along the scored lines with a sharp pair of scissors, remembering to leave a margin of $\frac{1}{2}$in (1.5cm) at one end of the copper so the strips remain held together as a whole sheet.

3 Cut the sheets of aluminum and brass into strips $\frac{1}{2}$in (1.5cm) wide and 14in (35cm) long. Butting the first strip up against the uncut edge of the copper, weave approximately 10 aluminum and 10 brass strips alternately through the copper.

4 Apply glue to each end of the aluminum and brass strips and press them firmly onto the copper to secure them in place.

5 For a neat finish, push over the protruding ends of the copper to give a clean edge.

Mysterious and magical as they glow in the dark, these copper, brass, and aluminum candleshades are woven from strips of the metal foil sheets. The warm, shiny, metallic surfaces reflect the flame, providing a warm and cheery light.

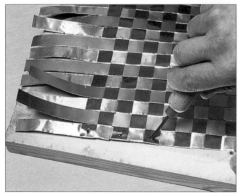

6 Punch three holes down each short edge of the woven sheet with a bradawl, making sure that the holes line up on each edge. Remember to use a wooden cutting board if you do not want to damage your work surface.

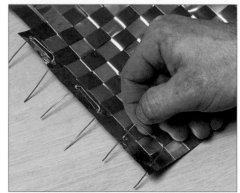

7 Cut three 4in (10cm) lengths of copper wire. Bring the two short edges of the woven foil together to form a cylinder and fasten them together by threading the wires through each set of punched holes and tying the ends together on the inside of the shade.

8 Finish the top of the candleshade by curling alternate strips of aluminum and brass under and over, using the end of a pen or pencil. To ensure that the candleshade sits level, trim the base with a pair of sharp scissors.

FLOWER-FILLED WAX BOX

*B*ECAUSE THIS LITTLE wax box is designed to hold a candle rather than to be burned, it is a decoration that will last for several years. Silk flowers are set within the wax casing, creating a bas-relief effect that looks stunning when illuminated from within. I have used artificial geraniums, with dyed pink wax, but this technique can be adapted with great success to look very effective with all sorts of flowers, leaves, and colors. I have also used dried herbs within sheets of white wax, which produces a more minimalist look. The one point to keep in mind is that the flowers, leaves, or herbs need to have a three-dimensional quality so they protrude a little through the wax; otherwise the exterior of your box will look flat and less interesting.

MAKING THE WAX BOX

You will need: silk flowers, such as carnations or geraniums; plastic tray as a mold; corrugated cardboard as a divider within the mold; paraffin wax; wax dye; double boiler; plasticizer; and a paintbrush (optional).

Melt a little extra wax so you have some left over to use to join the sides of the box together.

Cut up a piece of cardboard and divide your tray into square molds, each about 4sq.in (10sq.cm) in size.

1 Arrange a silk flower (or dried herb) in each of the square molds. If using more than one flower, group the flower heads into a central bunch. Melt the wax, then add dye and plasticizer.

2 Pour the molten wax mixture into the molds, being careful not to disturb the flowers. Do not cover the entire flower – some petals should stand above the wax.

3 Once the wax has set, after about three hours, remove the wax squares from the tray. Take a square, and dip one edge into the saucepan of left-over molten wax. Alternatively, dip a paintbrush into the wax and apply a coating to the edge of the square.

4 Place the wax-coated edge of one side of the square up to the edge of another to form the adjoining sides of the cube. Hold these pieces in place until the wax has set and the two sides are stuck together.

5 Repeat the process for the remaining three sides of the box. Once assembled, pour a small amount of molten wax into the cube and swirl it around to thinly coat the inside. This thoroughly seals all the edges. Turn the box upside down and pour any excess wax back into the saucepan.

Candles for the Kitchen

ECAUSE THE KITCHEN so often becomes the focus for the most successful parties and get-togethers, its decoration should be high on the list of priorities. The shiny surfaces of silver forks, cookie cutters, and aluminum bakeware are ideal for using in conjunction with candles since their reflective surfaces enhance and amplify the light of the flame. Making the most of the sculptural shapes of many kitchen utensils and gadgets, it is very easy to create fun and innovative candleholders for displaying around the kitchen, or on the table.

A B O V E *Simple cutlery is bent into an original design. A little essential oil is placed in the spoon, to be warmed by the candle underneath.*

L E F T *Votive candles sit in cookie cutters, and silver forks are used to support a beeswax candle, decorated with a collar of fresh thyme.*

47

WHISK HOLDER

*B*EING AN AVID cook, one of my favorite pastimes is to browse through the kitchen utensils on sale in gourmet cook shops in search of useful gadgets. The implements that generally catch my eye are those made from shiny chrome and steel, with sleek shapes that make them look more like contemporary sculptures than practical kitchen tools. There are many that could be incorporated into candle decorations, but one of my particular favorites is the standard whisk, which is available in a variety of sizes. Here I have combined a whisk with a couple of small, fluted tin molds, which are also very attractive little items on their own. Sold for use in pastry- and cake-making, they also happen to make ideal candleholders.

MAKING THE WHISK HOLDER

You will need: standard whisk; pair of metal molds; and glue gun or metal adhesive and a votive candle.

Although I have used a glue gun to attach the components here, if you want to make certain the bonding is secure and permanent, it is best to use a special metal adhesive.

Be careful not to touch the spokes of the whisk after the candle is lit because they will become hot.

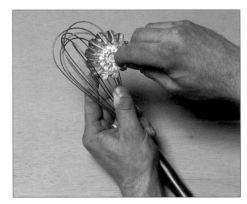

1 Gently pry the whisk spokes apart and push one of the tin molds into the cavity. Molds with fluted edges sit very snugly between the prongs.

2 To attach the mold, glue the spokes where they touch the sides of the mold. It is essential that the mold is secure because it will contain the candle.

3 Attach the second mold, upside-down, to the end of the whisk handle to create a stable base for the candleholder.

4 Add a votive candle to the holder and place it in a safe position where it is unlikely to be knocked over.

MAKING A HANGING WHISK HOLDER

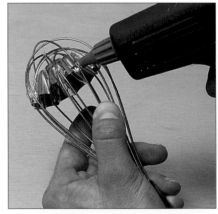

Use the whisk as a hanging holder by gluing the tin mold upside down to the top end of the whisk and suspending the whisk from its handle.

SPOON CANDLEHOLDER

*T*RADITIONAL WOODEN kitchen tools can be made into stunning candleholders – their clean lines and shapes echo the simplicity of ordinary candles, and the gentle tones of natural wood complement cream and white candles perfectly. This is a good way of using spoons and other utensils that have outlived their culinary purpose. Alternatively, secondhand stores usually sell a variety of old kitchenware. Tall and narrow, the candleholder will not take up too much room in the kitchen, and would look great on a windowsill or kitchen table. Here, I have used three wooden spoons – but wooden serving forks and even spatulas work just as well. In fact, just about any utensil will do, provided the wood is thick enough to hold a nail.

MAKING THE SPOON CANDLEHOLDER

You will need: three wooden spoons; thick candle; three nails, about 1in (3cm) long with small heads; hammer; and copper reel wire.

The nails need to be fairly sturdy to support the candle and take some of its weight once the finished holder is placed in an upright position.

For a different effect, you could make a wreath of fresh herbs, such as rosemary or thyme, and wire it around the bowls of the spoons.

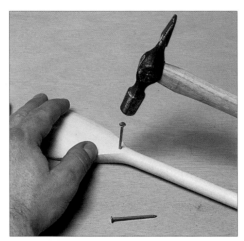

1 Hammer a nail two-thirds of the way through the back of each wooden spoon at the point where the handle meets the bowl. The nail should be secure but not visible from the other side.

2 Hold a spoon against the candle so that the base of the candle rests on the nail. Tightly bind the spoon onto the candle with the wire. Repeat with the other spoons, keeping the wire taut.

ROLLING PIN CANDLEHOLDER

Just to show that almost any kitchen utensil can be transformed into a candleholder, here is a traditional wooden rolling pin put to novel but very good use!

To keep the holder stable, use a file to create a flat surface on one side, and then drill three holes into the opposite side. A plain white household candle is then placed into each hole to finish the decoration.

ABOVE *This charming candleholder is made with three brand new wooden spoons. Inexpensive and easily constructed, it would make an impression in any kitchen.*

EGGSHELL CANDLES

*T*HESE RATHER quirky, whimsical candles are displayed in a wire egg rack and look marvelous in the kitchen. Great fun to make, they are an appropriate decoration for Easter, and children, if supervised, will find them fascinating. I have used extra-large chicken eggs, but if you are able to get them, goose eggs would be even better because they are so much larger. Unfortunately, these charming egg candles do not burn for very long because the shells only hold a small quantity of wax. You could also make whole egg-shaped candles, either using a purchased egg-shaped mold or a fresh egg that has been blown. For the latter, the wick is inserted through the blowing holes and the base sealed with mold seal. The top blowing hole is then enlarged slightly to allow molten wax (perhaps dyed an eggshell shade of beige) to be poured in. After the wax has set, the shell can be removed.

MAKING THE EGGSHELL CANDLES

You will need: fresh eggs and an egg carton; lengths of primed wick; paraffin wax; yellow wax dye; double boiler; small quantity of moss; wire egg rack; and a few quail's eggs to decorate the basket of the rack, if required.

Save the contents of the eggs in the bowl after cracking them open (you can use them in an omelet later!). Carefully wash the shells and place them upside down on some paper towels so they can drain and dry out before use.

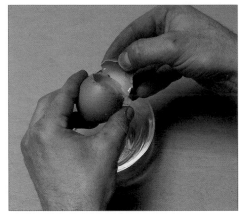

1 Crack open each of the eggs, breaking them toward one end to give you as much shell as possible and the maximum capacity for the wax.

2 Place the clean, dry eggshells into an egg carton to support them while making the candles. If you cannot use the egg carton, substitute eggcups.

3 Melt the paraffin wax and carefully pour it into the shells, so each one is at least two-thirds full. As it cools and sets, the wax will shrink slightly, making room for more wax.

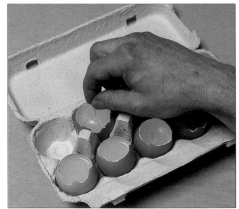

4 Cut a short piece of wick for each egg and, after a skin has formed on the surface of the wax, push the wick through it. As the wax sets it will support the wick.

5 Reheat the wax and dye it yellow (see Dyeing wax, page 12) to resemble egg yolk. Allow the dyed wax to cool slightly, then pour it into each egg, so it forms a small yolk-like pool.

Candles for the Garden and Conservatory

THERE IS SOMETHING *especially enchanting about watching dusk fall at the end of a perfect sunny day, and as the sun lowers, seeing its place taken by tiny candles within pots and paper bags, spaced around the plants and flowers. With terracotta pots and miniature galvanized buckets also making perfect holders for candles, the garden really comes alive after dark.*

ABOVE   *Tiny terracotta pots containing votive candles are suspended from bamboo canes arranged within an old-fashioned flowerpot.*

LEFT   *Colored paper bags protect the flames of small candles from early evening breezes and make a lovely display.*

55

TIN-CAN SCONCE

*U*SED YEARS AGO in the manufacture of many household objects, hardwearing tin was also utilized in conjunction with candles and other sources of light because it did not tarnish. Aluminum, its modern successor, is just as suitable for this project and is lightweight in addition to being particularly malleable. You could also recycle some well-washed-out food cans to make the sconce, although they will not be as shiny and are more difficult to work with – arm yourself with some tin snips for cutting and make sure you smooth any sharp edges with a file. Whichever form of can you choose, it will not cost much and the only other item needed is one little cabochon jewel. The end result is a decoration with a slightly Oriental feel, which looks effective indoors and out.

MAKING THE TIN-CAN SCONCE

You will need: one unopened soft-drink can; medium-grade steel wool; sharp, strong scissors; sheet of paper; adhesive tape; disposable ballpoint pen; a glass marble or large bead; and heat-resistant adhesive.

Wetting the can as you remove the printed design will help prevent static.

1 Use the steel wool to rub away at the printed design on the full soft-drink can. You will find that it comes off very easily, leaving a shiny, polished surface. Empty the contents of the can.

2 Cut off the top of the can with a pair of sharp scissors. Measure a piece of paper around the can and draw and cut out a pattern for the sconce. Attach it around the can and transfer the pattern onto the can, using the paper as a guide.

5 Using the heat-resistant glue, stick a bead, "jewel," or marble to the front of the sconce to act as a mirror which reflects the candlelight.

3 Remove the paper pattern, and then very carefully cut the can with the scissors, following the marked outline and taking care not to cut yourself on the sharp edge.

4 To add interest, mark a pattern of raised dots around the edge with a ballpoint pen. Use a wooden board as a work surface when making the indentations. You can also hammer in a small nail to pierce holes through the can, which results in a slightly different effect.

USING A FULL CAN

Once you have rubbed down the can (see step 1, left) you may drink the contents, but it is important to use a full, unopened can when rubbing off the printed motif because the aluminum is thin and will buckle easily under pressure.

R I G H T The little tin sconce, with a white votive candle dropped into its base, is nailed to a tree in the garden for an outdoor party. A number of sconces, hung from trees or shrubs outside or along a wall inside, create a magical effect.

PAPER BAG LANTERNS

*T*HESE SIMPLE PAPER bag lanterns could not be easier or less expensive to make, especially if you are on good terms with your local take-out restaurant! Many lanterns made using paper bags such as these, with patterns of holes pierced to decorate them, are available to buy from retail stores. I have made these slightly more individual by using a simple monogram as the decorative pattern, rather than punching holes. If you are making a large number of the lanterns, it is easiest to choose a fairly straightforward design. You can either draw your letters or design freehand, or find an idea that you like in a book, newspaper, or magazine and trace it.

MAKING THE PAPER BAG LANTERNS

You will need: paper bag, of the type used to pack containers of take-out foods; pencil; scalpel or craft knife; cutting board or mat; dry sand; and a votive candle in a glass holder for each bag.

When choosing your design, make sure it is reasonably delicate – if you cut too much paper from the center of the bag, it will weaken it – causing the bag to lose its shape.

1 With a pencil, draw your design onto one side of the bag, keeping it fairly central. If drawing two letters, space them a little apart to make cutting out easier.

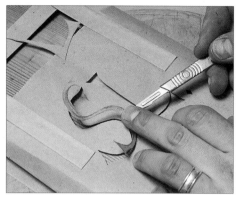

2 Place a cutting board inside the bag to prevent cutting through both sides of the paper. Using a craft knife, carefully cut out around the letters.

3 Remove the cutting board and open the bag, extending the seams. Spoon a little dry sand into the bag to weigh it down and keep it stable.

4 Place a small votive candle in a glass holder into the bag, pressing it into the sand. Make sure it is level and secure before lighting it.

STAR-MOTIF LANTERN

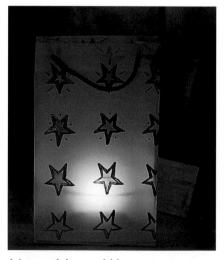

Many gift bags sold by stationery stores make ideal candle lanterns. Several stars have been cut out of this printed bag, creating a pretty effect.

TERRACOTTA POT STAND

OLD, WEATHERED flowerpots have great charm. Their warm, earthy colors and simple shapes make them ideal containers for all sorts of wonderful plants. They also happen to make very attractive candleholders, whether used individually or, as here, in a tall stack, made secure by a bamboo cane that runs through its middle. Old, rustic-looking terracotta flowerpots are increasingly fashionable, which means they are more difficult to find. If you cannot unearth any old clay flowerpots lurking in a forgotten corner of your greenhouse or shed, look out for them at garage sales and flea markets. Alternatively, buy new clay pots from a garden center or nursery and age them by rubbing dark tan shoe polish onto the terracotta with a soft cotton rag.

MAKING THE TERRACOTTA POT STAND

You will need: about seven small terracotta pots, which can be stacked inside one another, and one larger pot to form the base of the stack; length of bamboo cane or thin dowel stick; air-drying modeling clay; moss; and a pillar candle.

To make sure your candle stands upright in the top pot, pour in some sand or gravel to give it support.

1 Press three-quarters of the clay into the base of the largest pot, insert the cane into the center, and firm the clay around the cane to support it securely.

2 Place a smaller pot into base pot, threading it onto the cane through the drainage hole. Push the pot down so it rests on the clay.

3 Pack pieces of moss into the gap between the base pot and second pot. Press the moss in tightly to fill the gap between the two containers.

4 After the clay has set hard (see manufacturer's instructions), stack the remaining pots onto the cane. Cut off any extra cane at the top.

5 Press the rest of the clay around the tip of the cane in the top pot and leave to set. When dry, pour in sand or gravel and place a candle in the center.

Candles for the Bedroom

ITH THEIR WARM and subtle light, candles are a natural choice for the bedroom, casting a soft and flattering glow over the room – and its occupants. Pretty petal-covered candles and flowery candleshades add a delicate, feminine touch to a dresser or side table, while candles and candlestands decorated with glittering glass beads and jewels give a distinct feeling of glamour. The candlelit bedroom becomes a restful and romantic environment in which to relax and enjoy a little peace and tranquillity.

ABOVE *A glass drip holder is given a delicate and sparkling decorative treatment using crystal and glass beads from a broken necklace.*

LEFT *These simple translucent candles are embellished with pressed flowers, including scented lavender, and petals.*

ROSE CANDLESHADE

*T*HE GENTLE GLOW of candlelight is always enchanting, and even more so when filtered through this delicate shade. In Victorian England, candleshades were made from parchment, vellum, or paper and were said to cast a flattering glow on ladies' and gentlemen's faces as they dined. The shade rests on a metal bracket support, or embracer, usually made from brass or silver. This shade has an extra decorative dimension because it is covered with a frilly coat of individual dried rose petals, which have a beautiful translucency and give a warm rich light. As an added luxury I have made my shade from handmade paper that has had preserved flower petals added. When viewed from above or beneath the shade, the flecks of petals can be seen within the paper.

MAKING THE
ROSE CANDLESHADE

You will need: sheet of rigid paper or posterboard in a light color; 20-25 dried rose heads; double-sided tape; scissors; ballpoint pen; and flame-retardant spray.

A quick option is to decorate a purchased candleshade – or if you have an old shade, use it as a template for your posterboard or paper. Before use, spray the candleshade with flame-retardant spray. Make sure you keep the candle away from drafts and never leave the lit candle unattended.

1 Using the ballpoint pen, trace the outline of a candleshade onto your chosen sheet of posterboard or paper. Carefully cut out your template with a pair of sharp scissors.

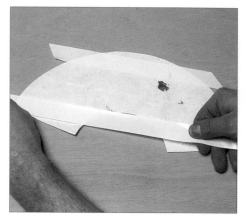

2 Completely cover one side of the cut-out paper with strips of double-sided adhesive tape. This provides a sticky surface for attaching the petals.

3 Gently dismantle the rose heads by separating out the individual petals. Beginning at the lower outer edge, press the dried rose petals in a neat row onto the double-sided adhesive tape, overlapping them slightly.

4 Gradually build up the rose petals row by row until the entire candleshade is covered with petals. Each row of rose petals should also slightly overlap the last.

5 Join the two edges of the candleshade with more double-sided adhesive tape, applying the tape to the inside of one edge and pressing down firmly on a hard surface.

USING A CANDLE EMBRACER

Candle embracers, or carriers, are
available from good department stores.
They must be used with a candle of the
correct diameter – usually a regular
household size. The embracer sits on
the top of the candle, and as the candle
burns, travels down with it. The
embracer will become warm when the
candle is lit, so handle with care and
never leave a burning candle unattended.

R I G H T *Warm and romantic, this*
paper shade covered with deep crimson
rose petals casts an enchanting glow
around a room.

BAROQUE CANDLESTICK

*G*LAMOROUS, wacky, and lots of fun, this candlestick is adorned with fake diamonds and pearls, glass beads, sequins, and plastic jewels. A simple metal candlestick forms the basis for this glittering decoration, dotted with touches of red and blue. You can embellish the candlestick with gems of your choice, whether shiny emeralds or sparkling sapphires! I have used beads and stones collected from craft stores, with "pearls" that are sold for use in bridal headdresses. Flea markets are also good sources of inexpensive sparkly materials.

MAKING THE
BAROQUE CANDLESTICK

You will need: simple metal candlestick; galvanized wire; wire cutters; assorted beads, necklaces, and plastic jewels; glitter; glue gun; stub wires, for the jewels; stars or sequins to decorate the candle; and a metal spoon with an insulated handle.

Simple metal candlesticks are available from retail stores, and you may be able to get a scratched one for a better price. It really doesn't matter what the candlestick looks like because it will be entirely covered.

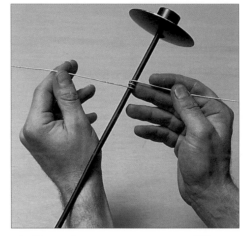

1 Using the wire cutters, snip off five 8in (20cm) lengths of galvanized wire. Bind each around the central stem of the candlestick, so the ends stick out like arms.

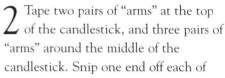
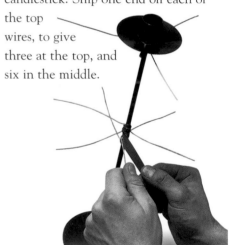

2 Tape two pairs of "arms" at the top of the candlestick, and three pairs of "arms" around the middle of the candlestick. Snip one end off each of the top wires, to give three at the top, and six in the middle.

3 Use the glue gun to apply adhesive to the base of the candlestick. Stick one end of the beads to it and wind the necklace up and around the stem to the top. Wind it back down a few turns to make the top look slightly wider than the base. Snip off the end and glue in place.

4 Attach stub wires to the larger jewels and secure them so that they hang from the protruding wire "arms." Wind more strings of beads around to completely cover the wires and then glue on more jewels and contrasting beads to create a highly decorative effect.

5 Attach another length of beads to the base of the candlestick with the glue gun. Add more jewels and sprinkle on sequins or glitter to cover the metal. Decorate the candle with stars or sequins using a warm spoon (for method see Petal-Covered Candle, page 68).

PETAL-COVERED CANDLE

*T*HIS IS A charming and simple idea that may be applied to any shape, size, or color of candle. I have used a large beeswax candle, because its pale honey coloring provides an ideal contrast to the soft pink zinnia petals around the sides, but you could experiment with many combinations of different colored flowers and candles. The real secret is to make sure that any of the flowers used are pressed, not simply dried, as they need to be able to lie as flat against the sides of the candle as possible. Pressed flowers can be obtained from some florists, but it is far less expensive to press your own – all you need is an old telephone book or two, some fresh flowers, and a couple of weights. Pressed leaves also look very effective, either added in among the flowers or used on their own.

MAKING THE PETAL-COVERED CANDLE

You will need: candle of your choice; pressed petals; saucepan; and a metal teaspoon with insulated handle.

If pressing your own flowers, flattish varieties, such as daisies and pansies, can be placed whole between the pages of a telephone book. Roses and multipetaled blooms should be preserved in parts; that is, the petals should be removed from the flower and pressed separately. Place the weights on top of the book and leave for a week.

1 Hold the teaspoon in a pan of boiling water for a few seconds to warm it up. Rub the back of the hot spoon against the candle to soften and melt the wax slightly.

2 Press a petal against the softened wax and hold it in place for several seconds, applying gentle pressure, until the wax has set.

3 Reheat the spoon in the boiling water, then gently rub the back of the spoon over the top of the petal and the surrounding area of wax. This will seal the petal within the wax, ensuring that it is securely attached.

4 Using the same technique, apply the pressed petals all around the circumference of the candle. You can use fewer petals for a simpler effect, or apply lots of petals and space them closer together for a more elaborate look.

ABOVE *Delicate pink zinnia petals, picked and pressed*
during the summer months, are used to decorate the
sides of a chunky cream beeswax candle, providing a reminder
of warm, sunny days.

Candles for the Bathroom

THE BATHROOM IS one place where the elements of fire and water coexist effectively. Together they can provide the perfect antidote to the stresses and strains of modern living; a hot bubble bath by flickering candlelight is the perfect way to unwind at the end of a long day. Candles can be used imaginatively to lend a touch of style and warmth to a room in which the lighting can often be rather harsh. Glowing through a beautiful shell wall sconce, flickering on shelves or ledges around the bath, or floating in water, candles can show the bathroom in an entirely new light.

A B O V E *These simple, delicately fluted scallop shell candles add a romantic touch to the bathroom.*

L E F T *Strings of tiny shells are threaded together to form garlands that add the finishing touch to this shell-encrusted wall sconce.*

71

SHELL WALL SCONCE

*T*HE HEIGHT OF relaxation is to bathe by candle-light, and such indulgence is made all the easier by this shell-encrusted wall sconce, which safely holds a small candle, shading its flame with a fluted scallop shell. I have always had a fascination for sea shells and find it impossible to pass them by as I walk along the shore. As a result, I possess a substantial collection with which to create such projects! I would heartily recommend collecting shells from the beach while on vacation, as they can be expensive to buy. Another way of obtaining interesting shells is to ask your local fish dealer or seafood restaurant to save you some. Be warned, however; they may come with garlic and butter and need a good wash with bleach and hot water before use!

MAKING THE SHELL WALL SCONCE

You will need: wrought-iron wall sconce, available from retail stores; selected shells in a variety of sizes; glue gun and sticks of glue; and starfish.

Strings of small shells cover the base of the sconce quickly and easily. Alternatively, small shells or even fine-grade gravel glued over the sconce will provide a base onto which you can add larger shells.

1 Wind a string of shells around the arm of the iron wall sconce until it is completely covered, and then glue the ends into place.

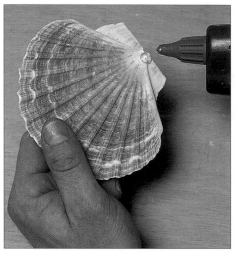

2 Using a hot glue gun, apply adhesive to a large scallop shell and attach it to the top of the sconce. Attach a second shell to the base.

3 Add a third shell to act as a shade on the candle bowl. Scallop shells are ideal for this purpose, as they are large, yet allow light to pass through.

4 Add more shells in different shapes and sizes, keeping in mind that the finished sconce should look balanced when attached to the wall.

5 A dried starfish is glued to the front of the decoration. After the sconce is screwed to the wall, a shell or two may be added to disguise any nails.

SHELL CANDLES

*T*HE DELICATE CONTOURS and coloring of shells can be enjoyed and appreciated up close when they are used as candleholders. Because shells tend to be relatively shallow, it is advisable to choose the largest you can find because the more wax you can fit into them, the longer they will burn.

Fluted scallop shells make attractive holders, as do mussel shells, which have a natural blue, opalescent finish. You could also use oyster shells, or even conches – the latter are particularly effective because they hold more substantial quantities of wax. If using conches, it is important to make sure you place the wick securely within the shell. Shell candles can be created in a wide variety of colors. Here, I have used plain paraffin wax – but soft, pastel shades look very pretty and effectively highlight the natural beauty of the shells, while strong, bright colors add a dramatic touch to the bathroom.

After the candles have burned down, just clean the shells and refill them with fresh wax and wicks so they can be enjoyed time and time again.

MAKING THE SHELL CANDLES

You will need: selection of large, flat shells (such as scallop, oyster, or mussel shells); paraffin wax; double boiler; wax dye (if required) and primed wick.

Before using the shells as containers, make sure that they are thoroughly clean and dry.

1 It is important that the shells have a level base, otherwise the wax will run out of the shell when the candle is burning and make a mess. If a shell is unstable, shave its base with a metal file to create a flat surface.

2 Stick the shells to a metal baking sheet using molding wax so that they remain in a secure position while the wax is being poured in.

3 Melt the paraffin wax over a double boiler and then carefully pour hot wax into the shells, filling them right to the rim.

4 Once the wax has semi-set, insert a primed wick, trimmed to fit the shell candle. Top up with molten wax and leave to set for about 1-2 hours.

FLOATING CANDLES

T HE IDEA OF relaxing in a bath, surrounded by tiny candles floating on the water's surface is one that holds a certain appeal. On a practical level, however, it is not a therapy I would recommend, since the average-sized bath would make this a dangerous experience! The next best solution is to place a bowl of floating candles near the bath so you are able to watch them gently drift on the surface of the water, safe in the knowledge that you do not risk suffering any burns. For this project, I have used an ordinary baking pan as a mold. In fact, you can use almost any container, provided it has a suitable shallow shape. All candles will float, since wax is a buoyant substance, but they have to be relatively flat in order to float in an upright position.

MAKING THE FLOATING CANDLES

You will need: standard muffin pan; vegetable oil; paraffin wax; assorted wax dyes; double boiler; stearin; primed wicks; and a metal spatula.

Before pouring wax into the pan, grease the insides of each mold with a small amount of vegetable oil. This will make it much easier to remove the candles from the tray after the wax has set. Trim a primed wick into short lengths to just above the height of the baking pan.

1 Dye your first batch of molten wax (see page 12) and pour into the pan, filling each mold to just below the rim. Continue with assorted colors.

2 When the wax has set slightly and feels tacky to the touch, carefully insert the trimmed wicks into the center of each candle.

3 Once the candles have set, after about 2-3 hours, slide the metal spatula gently around the edge of each mold to loosen each candle before levering it out.

VARIATIONS ON A FLOATING THEME

Tiny floating candles look very pretty in the bathroom, especially when displayed in an attractive glass vase or bowl. They can be dyed to coordinate with the decor or to suit a mood – the cool purple and blue tones (right) are very calming. Why not sprinkle seashells or pebbles on the bottom of the container to reflect the ocean theme, or float fresh flowerheads and leaves among the candles on the water's surface?

Celebrating with Candles

T HE MAGICAL GLOW of candlelight adds an extra dimension to any event, whether a dinner party, birthday, anniversary, or even afternoon tea. In fact, candles can really light up a celebration by providing instant atmosphere. There are some wonderful candles now available in department stores at certain times of the year, such as at Christmas and Halloween – but with a little know-how it is easy to create your own innovative and unusual displays, giving that all-important occasion a more personal, thoughtful touch.

A B O V E   *Brightly colored glass vases make vibrant candleholders for an evening garden party.*

L E F T   *Large glass vases are filled with layers of crumbled wax that has been dyed in contrasting shades of color, resembling giant exotic cocktails.*

79

CRUMBLED WAX GLASSES

*T*HIS IS A FUN way to make stunning candles from ground-up wax. The beauty of the technique is that it allows for endless variety because you can use clear containers of all shapes and sizes, and produce a wide range of effects. Experiment with distinctive bands of color, change shade gradually and subtly, or add glitter – the only limit is your imagination! You will need an old coffee bean grinder for this project since the wax can be difficult to remove entirely and may taint the flavor of your coffee. Grind the wax in short bursts to prevent it from melting and clogging the machine. An old paintbrush is useful for cleaning the grinder between batches.

MAKING THE CRUMBLED WAX GLASSES

You will need: old coffee grinder; wax chips; wax dye or colored wax; glitter (optional); selection of glasses; and primed wick.

When making up batches of crumbled wax, work on one color or wax type at a time and store the leftovers in a jar for future use. The chips may eventually form a large, hard lump, but you can easily loosen them again. Simply place the sealed jars of wax in the freezer for a few hours, remove and shake the jars, and the wax will separate into crumbs.

1 Place a couple of handfuls of wax chips into the coffee grinder. Do not attempt to grind larger amounts of wax because this will clog the machine. Add colored wax or glitter when required.

2 Grind the wax chips in the coffee grinder for just a few seconds – after grinding, they should have a texture resembling coarse sea salt.

3 Carefully spoon the ground wax into your chosen glass, filling it to within about 3/8in (1cm) of the top. If you are using different colored waxes, add a little of each color at a time.

4 Trim a length of primed wick to the height of the glass, then simply push the wick down into the middle of the crumbled wax.

COLORED WAX GLASSES

Wax left over from other projects, scraps of colored candles, or even broken wax crayons can all be recycled to add color to the crumbs.

GIFT CANDLE

*T*HIS IS A MARVELOUS way to transform a plain, square candle into a glamorous and expensive-looking gift box. Inside, I can just imagine a little jewel-encrusted brooch or bracelet, boxed and gift-wrapped by a top jeweler! The colors used here are combinations of pale and bright pink, and green and purple, which provide an attractive contrast. However, you can choose your own favorite color combinations. A point to keep in mind is that this style of decorated candle tends to work much better on a smaller scale. After you have mastered the technique, you can design your own individual and unique patterns and finishes. The flexible molding wax can be adapted to a range of different gift-wrapping ideas, limited only by your imagination!

MAKING THE GIFT CANDLE

You will need: cube-shaped candle, about 3¹/₄in (8cm) square; paraffin wax; wax dye in your chosen colors; double boiler; colored molding wax; sharp knife; cutting board; paintbrush; rolling pin; and a wooden skewer. Although a cube-shaped candle has been used here, cylindrical and pillar-shaped candles can be turned into gift boxes.

Soften the molding wax sheets according to the instructions on the package (usually this means placing the sheet in a bowl of hot water for up to five minutes).

1 Paint the molten, dyed paraffin wax onto the candle, gradually building up the coats until the desired shade and depth of color is achieved.

2 Roll out the softened wax into thin sheets, about ¹/₈ in (3mm) thick. Cut the wax into strips to form 10 lengths of "ribbon."

3 Press the wax strips onto the candle. The warmth of your hands should help them stick – or you could also apply a small amount of molten wax as glue.

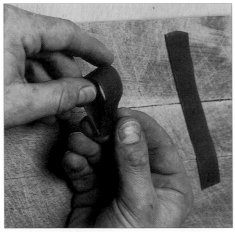

4 Make four bows by bending four strips of wax in half and pressing the two ends together. Position the bows around the wick.

5 Make the bow ends from two wax strips. Cut out a tiny wax square, skewer a hole in the center, and thread it over the wick. Press to hide any seams.

CHILDREN'S PARTY HOLDERS

*T*HESE BRIGHTLY COLORED candleholders will appeal to children of all ages – or to anyone with a sweet tooth! I based this idea on the silver foil balls studded with sticks of cheese and fruit that were so popular at parties during the seventies. For this nineties' version, I have used spheres of foil-wrapped dried florists' foam, replacing the cheese and fruit with lots of colorful candy. You could use colored tissue paper instead of the foil, using a little glue to hold it in place around the florists' foam.

MAKING THE CHILDREN'S PARTY HOLDERS

You will need: dried florists' foam spheres; dinner candles; sharp knife; aluminum foil or colored tissue paper; wooden skewers or toothpicks; and assorted candy.

1 Slice off the bottom of a dried florists' foam sphere to create a level base and wrap it in aluminum foil, making sure the sphere is completely covered.

2 Stand the sphere on a flat surface and place a candle centrally on the top. Score around the candle base with a knife. Using a melon baller, scoop out the foam from the marked area to two-thirds of the way down the sphere and insert the candle.

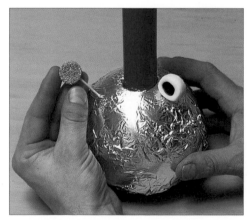

3 Break a number of wooden skewers in half and spear assorted candy onto the ends. Push the other ends into the dried foam, covering the sphere with the candy. Lollipops can be pushed directly into the sphere.

84

WAX SPONGE CAKE

*T*HIS DELICIOUS-LOOKING orange sponge cake, decorated with crystallized orange slices and drizzled with icing, is actually made using natural beeswax, orange and yellow molding wax, and a cake ring mold. A fun centerpiece at a tea party or birthday celebration, the natural colors of the beeswax are ideally suited to this project. You could also adapt this easy technique to make gorgeous "cakes" in just about every flavor – by adding dark brown wax dye to your molten mixture, for example, to cook up an extremely convincing "chocolate" gâteau! The same method works just as well on a smaller scale, to make individual buns, cupcakes, and tarts. Just be careful that your guests do not take a bite from them by mistake!

MAKING THE WAX CAKE

You will need: metal ring mold, nonstick and about 9¹/₂in (24cm) in diameter; natural and bleached beeswax; paraffin wax; stearin; primed wick; double boiler; sheets of molding wax in orange and yellow; chopping board, knife; and a rolling pin.

Melt the natural beeswax over a double boiler, adding one part paraffin wax and ¹/₂ part stearin to every 5 parts beeswax. The paraffin wax makes the beeswax lighter in color and more translucent, and the stearin helps in releasing the set candle from the mold.

1 Fill the ring mold two-thirds full with the natural beeswax, stearin, and paraffin wax mixture and leave to set for about three hours. Release it from the mold and place on a covered surface.

2 Make four holes in the ring with a wicking needle and insert primed wicks. Melt some bleached beeswax, stir, and allow to cool slightly. Pour the wax over the "cake" to resemble icing.

3 Roll the yellow molding wax into a sausage shape and the orange wax into a flat sheet. Wrap the sheet around the "sausage," and smooth the seam.

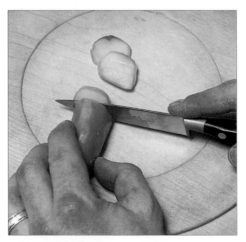

4 Make sure the wax roll is even in shape and then cut it into slices with a knife. Using the back of the knife, mark out the fruit "sections."

5 Decorate the ring with these "fruit slices," both whole and cut into halves. They will stick onto the cake if slightly warmed in your hands.

GLASS BOTTLE CANDLEHOLDERS

*A*NY ATTRACTIVE, interesting-looking bottles are ideal for this project, provided they have necks wide enough to accommodate a standard candle. Mineral and spring waters in particular, seem to come in a wide range of unusual bottles these days – so you may find that you can gather a good selection of shapes and sizes from the supermarket shelf. This is a colorful and inexpensive decoration for a party, and is very appropriate for young people. You can choose your colors to suit your party theme, even adding glitter and sequins to the water to add an extra sparkle.

1 Mix up water with a few drops of food coloring or ink and stir. Pour the various colored waters into the bottles, filling them to just over half-full.

2 Insert your candles into the bottles or, for thicker candles, trim them to fit the necks of the bottles.

MAKING THE GLASS BOTTLE CANDLEHOLDERS

You will need: selection of clear glass bottles, in a variety of shapes, heights, sizes, and styles; food coloring and ink; and brightly colored candles.

Choose your color scheme for the candles and holders and extend it to balloons, streamers, and other party paraphernalia to create a stunning effect.

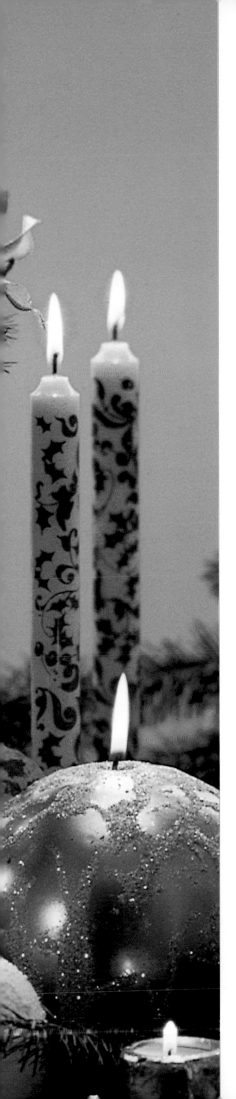

Christmas and Thanksgiving

*T*HE FESTIVE SEASON *is the time of year to go overboard on candle decorations, for they are as much a part of the celebrations as the tree, the turkey, and other trimmings. There is a vast selection of Christmas candles available from retail stores, from wax Santa Claus figures to glittery ornaments, but it is always satisfying and fun to supplement your purchased decorations with a few homemade displays. Count down to Christmas with an Advent candle, create a beautiful candlelit wreath or a pretty stained glass holder – this chapter contains a wealth of ideas to help you celebrate in style.*

A B O V E *Miniature pumpkin candles, arranged on autumnal leaves, are perfect for a Thanksgiving dinner table.*

L E F T *A pine, holly, and trailing ivy wreath holds fragrant green candles among gold ribbons, while festive candles beneath provide a warm glow.*

LOG AND FRUIT HOLDERS

*T*HIS SIMPLE IDEA makes use of natural ingredients to create beautiful candleholders on an autumnal theme, which would be particularly appropriate for a Halloween or Thanksgiving celebration. A slender birch tree trunk is cut into short lengths, and the base of each length is filed so it sits level. A drill is then used to create a cavity in the other end, into which votive candles, or even taller candles, may be placed. The apple votive holders are a great favorite at parties, and I often place a cluster of them around a fresh arrangement of flowers at the dinner table to add an extra decorative element to the centerpiece. You may use red or green apples, but they should be unbruised and as shiny and firm as possible.

MAKING THE LOG AND FRUIT HOLDERS

You will need: length of natural tree branch, as straight as possible; electric drill and ¹/₄in (6mm) drill bit attached into a hole saw; sharp chisel; apples; sharp knife; melon baller; and votive candles.

When pruning trees, keep any thicker branches in a dry, covered place so you can use them later as candleholders. Alternatively, many nurseries and garden centers sell rustic poles, with their natural bark covering still intact, for building arbors and other structures.

1 After filing the base of the branch to make it level, place it on a flat surface (or in a vise) and position the drill in the center of the top end.

2 Holding the branch firmly with one hand, carefully use the electric drill to carve out a cavity, approximately 1in (2.5cm) deep.

3 Chisel out the plug of wood within the drilled area, making the base as level as possible so the candle will sit flat when inserted into the hole.

REMOVING FLESH FROM THE APPLES

Cut a slice from the bottom of the apple so it is level. Press a votive candle upside down on the top of the apple to make a mark, and cut around the indentation with a knife. With the melon baller, remove the flesh within the scored circle, so the candle fits snugly inside.

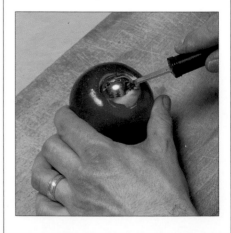

92

ADVENT RING

*T*RADITIONALLY LIT on each of the four Sundays leading up to Christmas day, Advent candles are a wonderful way of celebrating and welcoming the festive season. This old custom is still very much alive and practiced in homes and churches throughout the world. At a time of year when commercialism is so prevalent that it seems in danger of taking over, it is refreshing to harken back to the simpler ways of heralding in this magical time of year.

Here, I have taken the old favorite of an Advent ring and combined it with two more traditional ideas. One has its origins in Scandinavia, where the coming of Christmas is marked with celebrations that include the crowning of a young girl with a headdress of evergreen foliage and candles. The other is derived from the Christingle, a Christian service in Great Britain held for children in the days before Christmas, in which each child is presented with a decorated fruit with a lighted candle in it. Two versions of this ring could also be made to celebrate Hanukkah, the eight-day Jewish festival of lights which commemorates the rededication of the temple by Judas Maccabaeus in 165 B.C.

RIGHT *The dark green, clipped boxwood foliage provides an excellent contrast to the rich and vibrant colors of oranges and cranberries. One red candle is lit each weekend during the Advent season.*

MAKING THE ADVENT RING

You will need: florists' foam-filled plastic wreath frame (these are available from garden centers and craft stores); two lengths of strong galvanized wire; reel wire; florists' stub wires; a quantity of boxwood foliage, or selected evergreen foliage; scissors; four tall dinner candles; four oranges; fresh cranberries (optional); wooden skewers; and an apple corer.

To secure the fruit and candles in the foam wreath, push three short pieces of wire into the base of each orange to form a tripod before inserting the candles into the foam. The fruit then sits on the tripod, just above the wet foam, which prevents it from rotting.

1 Break the stems of boxwood into shorter pieces, about 5in (12cm) long. Insert the stems of boxwood into the foam, working around the ring in one direction. Make sure you cover the edge of the plastic tray as you work.

2 After you have covered the ring, trim off any straggly pieces of boxwood with scissors. Cut two lengths of thick wire, each 1$\frac{1}{2}$ times the diameter of the hole in the center. Using fine reel wire and more small sprigs of boxwood, bind them along the length of the wire until each is covered.

3 Insert the two boxwood-covered wires into the foam ring to form an elevated cross within the center of the wreath. Use stub wires to anchor these crosspieces into the foam within the frame.

4 Remove a plug from the center of the fruit with the apple corer and insert the candles, pushing them through the base of each orange so they protrude by about 3in (7cm). Push the candle and wired fruit (see Making the Advent Ring) firmly into the foam base.

ADVENT CANDLE

This simple Advent candle is created using a bought candle and sheets of modeling wax, cut into bands to represent 25 days of December. The candle is burned down one level each evening.

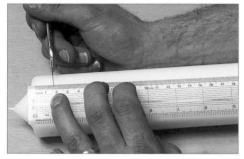

1 Using a ruler and a craft knife, make small indentations down the length of the candle to denote 25 days, allowing at least ³/₄in (1.5cm) between each level.

2 Mark out 24 strips of colored wax at least 5mm (¹/₅in) wide and cut them with the knife and ruler. Keep them cool until you are ready to use them.

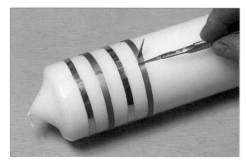

3 Press the wax strips onto the candle at the marked intervals. Here, two shades of gold are alternated to add interest. Trim off the excess with a knife.

GLASS JEWEL SPIRE

T HE SIMPLEST ideas can often turn out to be the most effective, as this little jewel spire clearly demonstrates. It was inspired by the the conical wrought-iron candlestand (shown far right), which I have recreated on a much smaller scale, using easily obtainable, basic materials. Once the wire frame has been constructed, it is adorned with clear glass beads that glimmer elegantly, reflecting the flame of the candle. Do keep in mind that the wire will conduct heat, so it will become very hot when the candle is lit. For this reason these spires should be kept away from children and should always be placed on a heat-resistant surface.

MAKING THE SPIRE

You will need: three 12in (30cm) lengths and one 24in (60cm) length of medium-gauge galvanized wire; medium-gauge and fine silver reel wire; selection of glass beads and "jewels;" needle-nose pliers; wire cutters; and a pencil.

Within the spire, I have used a thick, frosted cream-colored candle to add a wintry feel to the finished decoration. If you have any leftover materials, you can make a few miniature spires – these look very effective when placed over votive candles.

1 Shape the longest wire into a cone spiral, bending it with your hands so it resembles a spring. Start with a tiny circle, making each ring larger until the spire is about 10in (25cm) high.

2 Secure the two ends of the last and largest spiral with reel wire, winding it around tightly several times to join the ends neatly. This will hold the galvanized wire firmly in place.

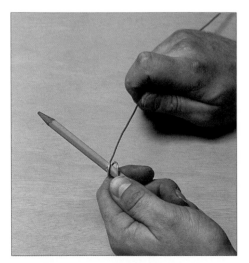

3 Make three round 'feet' from short lengths of wire. Wind each length twice around a pencil and then remove the pencil.

4 Fix the supports (feet at the bottom) to the frame, weaving each support in and out of alternate spirals and binding with reel wire at each join.

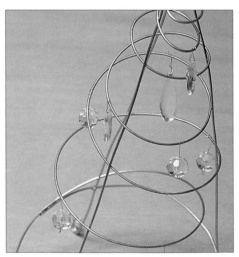

5 Bind the three supports together at the top with reel wire and then thread glass beads onto short lengths of reel wire and hang them from the spiral.

MAGICAL LIGHTS

This imposing, wrought-iron candlestand makes a wonderful floor-standing decoration. Glass stars and "jewels" are suspended from the frame, reflecting the glow of the votive candles as they burn within frosted glass.

STAINED GLASS HOLDER

*W*HEN THE INTERIOR of a church is lit up and the glow can be seen through stained glass windows, the effect is especially magical. Much of the stained glass seen today features bright jewel-like colors, such as green, red, and blue, which were incorporated into the glass at the smelting stage. The glass was then cut, and strips of lead were shaped around each piece of glass. It is simple to recreate this stained-glass effect, since many art and craft stores stock glass paints that give excellent results. If you have not used glass paints before, choose a straight-sided container, because you will find it much easier to to draw and paint onto a flat surface.

MAKING THE STAINED GLASS HOLDER

You will need: cube-shaped glass vase or jar; lead-colored outline paint; stained glass paints in red, green, yellow, and blue; fine paintbrush; paintbrush cleaner or turpentine to clean the brush; gold size; and two sheets of imitation gold leaf.

I have used a simple design, based on a traditional stained glass window. Whatever design you choose, keep in mind that you will have to paint the gaps in between, so give yourself enough room to maneuver.

1 Using the outline paint, draw a grid onto each side of the jar, leaving the paint to dry for a few minutes between applications. When completed, let the outline paint dry for several hours.

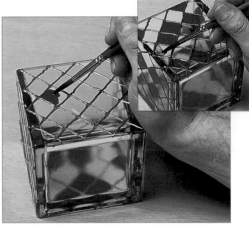

2 Apply glass paint sparingly to the "squares." Use one color at a time to build up a pattern, allowing each coat to dry before moving the container. Leave 2-3 squares empty on each side.

3 Carefully apply a thin layer of gold size to the unpainted squares and leave for about 15 minutes until it is tacky. This forms an adhesive surface for the gold leaf. Be careful not to splash the outline paint with gold size, or the gold leaf will stick to that, too.

4 Break off small pieces of gold leaf and gently press them onto the sized squares. Use a soft, dry paintbrush to smooth the gold leaf over the surface.

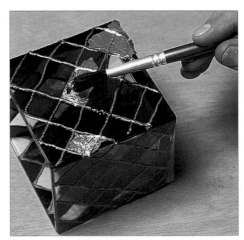

5 Using the dry brush, carefully remove any excess gold leaf. It will brush off easily, so be careful not to rub it off the sized squares in the process.

Candles as Gifts

CANDLES ALWAYS MAKE popular presents, and by adding your own personal touches and using clever and original ways in which to wrap, decorate, and present them, the gift will be enhanced even more. Pastel-colored candles look even prettier placed among coral pink tissue paper in a simple box, while several lime green candles tied with cheerful gingham ribbon make a charming bundle. By presenting candles in an attractive glass bowl, vase, or even a garden box, you can be certain that, when the last flickering flame has died, a use will always be found for the container in which the candles came.

A B O V E   *An ideal Easter present, this whitewashed garden box is filled with cheerful yellow "egg" candles placed on a bed of fresh moss.*

L E F T   *Fresh-looking ribbons, papers, tissues, and boxes can transform even simple household candles into an attractive and original gift.*

WRAPPING CANDLES

*T*HESE FUN ideas for wrapping and presenting candles are extremely simple, but they make the gifts just that little bit extra special. The large square candle (below) has its own match holder and emery board attached within a green canvas trimming and would be ideal for a male friend. The floating candle bowl (right) contains all the elements necessary for the enjoyment of the candles, from an attractive glass bowl to the water that should be poured into it! You could also make a present of a single floating candle in a smaller bowl filled with shells, pebbles, and pieces of sea-washed glass, adding a label with the words "just add water" in place of the water bottle. The little wish boxes (far right) can be decorated with many emblems – such as simple horoscope symbols, for example – and are an inexpensive yet charming way of giving away small candles.

MAKING THE MATCH HOLDER TRIMMING

You will need: large candle; canvas webbing; plastic bottle top; glue gun; scissors; matches; and an emery board.

This canvas trim and match holder is designed for use with a fairly substantial candle that has a relatively long burning time. Alternatively, you could attach the holder and trimming to an attractive ceramic pot or candleholder and place a candle inside. The candle could then be replaced and the matches replenished when necessary.

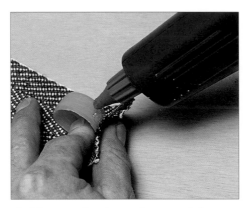

1 Measure the circumference of the candle and the bottle top and add 2 in (5cm). Cut a length of webbing to this measurement and then wrap one end of the material around the bottle top, attaching it with a glue gun.

2 Starting just off-center on one side, stick the webbing to the base of the candle with the glue gun, ensuring the fabric is pulled tight around the corners.

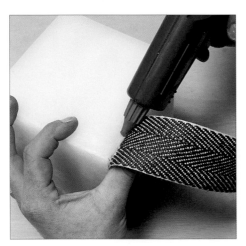

3 Work around the sides of the candle, pressing the fabric firmly so it sits flat against the wax, until you return to the point where you started.

4 Finally, glue the covered bottle top into place, flush against the side of the candle, so it covers the seam. Fill the holder with matches and an emery board to use as a flint.

MAKING THE FLOATING CANDLE BOWL

You will need: suitable bowl (glass, ceramic, or otherwise); marbles, pebbles, or shells; floating candles (see pages 76-77), glitter or stars; a bottle containing enough water to allow the candles to float; and food coloring (optional).

1 Place the marbles or shells into your chosen bowl and then add a scattering of glitter or stars.

2 Position the floating candles in an attractive pattern on top of the marbles and glitter.

3 Place the bottle of water in the bowl, having added a little food coloring to give it a subtle shade if desired. Wrap the bowl in a cloud of cellophane (below), placing a pad of tissue paper beneath the bowl to protect it. Finish with a ribbon bow.

MAKING THE WISH BOXES

You will need: small boxes, able to take a small, foil-cased votive candle; small sponge; pen; sharp craft or modeling knife; scissors; poster paints; foil-cased votive candles; cellophane or tissue paper; ribbon; and scented essential oil (optional).

1 Cut the sponge into pieces large enough for your design and, using a pen, draw an emblem onto each.

2 With the knife and scissors, cut away the excess sponge around each emblem to create a printing block.

3 Mix the paint in an old saucer, dip in the sponge block, and lightly but firmly apply to the lid of the box.

4 Place the candle in the box, add a few drops of scented oil, if desired, and wrap in tissue paper or cellophane.

EXOTIC CANDLES

*A*N UNUSUAL AND interesting gift idea, this decoration was inspired by a trip to India, and certainly makes an original alternative to a bottle of wine or a bunch of flowers. The votive candles used within it are known by many names, including nightlights, tea lights, and calorettes. They are called votive candles because they are used as religous offerings during Roman Catholic mass.

In effect, these are simply small self-contained candles made within their own aluminum holders. Relatively safe to use, in pre-electricity days they were often placed in the nursery or a small child's bedroom at night. They are extremely useful to have around the home because they are incredibly versatile.

Here I have used them within a striking motif of colored sand in a shallow terracotta dish, an idea based on similar offerings I saw in many of the temples while traveling through Rajasthan in northwest India. The sand makes a stable base in which the candles nestle securely, and a sprinkling of marigold petals provides a colorful finishing touch.

ABOVE *Votive candles are dotted among the swirled patterns in the sand and delicate marigold petals are scattered in a circle, making this a different and imaginative way of presenting candles.*

MAKING THE EXOTIC CANDLES

You will need: suitably sized shallow saucer, made from terracotta, tough plastic, or other material in a color that complements the other ingredients; quantity of sand, colored if desired; small aluminum-cased votive candles; and fresh flower petals.

Instead of using sand, you could also try filling the dish with either fine gravel or coarse sea salt, as both of these look very effective. For a more colorful result, aquarium gravel, which is sold for use in fish tanks, comes in a wide range of colors. Perhaps you could use up any leftovers after making the Chunky Gravel Candle (see page 18).

1 Make sure that the saucer is dry, and then carefully pour in the sand. If you are using two or more colors, pour in one at a time to create the pattern of your choice. Do not overfill the dish.

2 Use your finger or a short piece of dowel to form interesting patterns and swirls throughout the different colors of sand.

3 Position the votive candles in the sand-filled saucer. Place each one on the surface of the sand and then gently push the candle down, rotating it slightly so most of the foil casing is buried.

4 Add a sprinkling of fresh flower petals, placing them well away from wicks of the candles. You could also add whole small flower heads among the candles, such as rosebuds, primroses, or Singapore orchids.

WRAPPED VOTIVES

When decorating tables for parties, I have found that many venues that do not allow candles as part of the table setting will permit the use of these votives if they are placed within special heat-resistant glass holders, such as the ones used here.

By wrapping the glass containers with different materials, from fresh or preserved leaves and slices of fruit to lengths of ribbon or pieces of fabric, all sorts of original effects are achieved. Here I have opted for a very delicate covering, using skeletonized magnolia leaves and a sheer, gold-embossed ribbon, secured in place with gold and silver reel wire, to decorate the holders.

1 Press a single leaf, here a skeletonized magnolia leaf, against the side of the glass jar. Position a second leaf so it slightly overlaps the first.

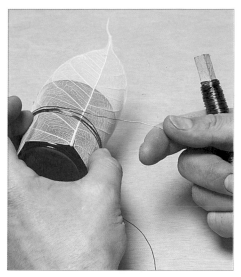

2 Using silver or gold wire, bind it around the glass holder a couple of times to attach the leaves into place. Twist the two wires together and trim.

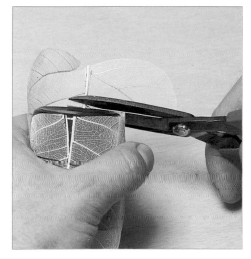

3 Trim off the leaf around the top of the jar with a pair of scissors. This will ensure that the leaves will not catch fire when the candle is lit.

RIGHT *Illuminated by flickering candlelight, the delicate leaf- and ribbon-wrapped holders look extremely pretty.*

109

INDEX

ACKNOWLEDGMENTS

This book is the sum total of a great deal of creativity and hard work by many people, and without their talents and generosity of spirit it could never have come into being.

I would like to thank Susan Berry, of Collins & Brown, for believing in the concept. Her care of both the book's development and mine has made working upon this title an interesting, entertaining, and greatly enjoyable process.

Many thanks to the editor, Mandy Lebentz for knocking both the book (and sometimes me!) into a cohesive and workable form. Her presence at photo shoots and her calming and understanding manner have made my life much easier while working on this title, and to her I am truly grateful. Michelle Garrett, assisted by the ever-steadfast Dulcie, has made our days of photography fun, innovative, and greatly enjoyable. Michelle's wonderfully robust philosophies and her caring and thoughtful conversations mark her out as a very special person with whom I am honoured to have worked.

While I have been devoting much of my time to this title, my workroom and its staff have been continuing to create the floral decorations for events large and small throughout the country. It is greatly reassuring for me to know that in my absence the standard of work upon which our reputation is founded continues to flourish. Without the hard work and care taken by Jon Poulsom and Ruth Harris, my workload would have become unbearable. Others who must also be thanked for giving of their time and talents so generously are Jaynie Heynes, Darryn McColl, Roy Steptoe, and Pat Mitchell with her ever-attentive flock; Angie, Paul, and the two Grants.

Lastly, my thanks must always go to Nicholas, and he will know why.